The legacy of World War II

Author: Seidlitz, Lauri.
Reading Level: 6.9 MG
Point Value: 1.0
ACCELERATED READER QUIZ 179903
Lexile Value: 920L

WORLD WAR II

HISTORY'S DEADLIEST CONFLICT

THE LEGACY
— OF —
WORLD WAR II

CATHOLIC WORKER

LET'S DO IT
GANDHI'S WAY
-NOT TRUMAN'S

YOUR TAXES
PAY FOR THE
H-BOMB

LAURI SEIDLITZ

 Crabtree Publishing Company
www.crabtreebooks.com

Author: Lauri Seidlitz

Publishing plan research and development: Crabtree Publishing Company

Editors: Jackie Dell, Lynn Peppas

Proofreaders: Kelly Stern, Wendy Scavuzzo

Editorial services: Clarity Content Services

Production coordinator and prepress technician: Tammy McGarr

Print coordinator: Margaret Amy Salter

Series consultant: Fayaz Chagani

Cover design: Ken Wright

Design: David Montle

Photo Research: Linda Tanaka

Front cover: Nuclear weapon test of hydrogen bomb Mike

Title page: Protest against the use of tax dollars for the development of nuclear weapons

Contents page "Rosie the Riveter" poster used by the United States government to encourage women to work in factories building war supplies; Emperor Hirohito and U.S. General Douglas MacArthur

Photo Credits:
Front cover: Wikimedia: Public Domain; Back cover: Wikimedia: public domain
Title page Library of Congress/World-Telegram/photo by F. Palumbo; p3t US Gov/War Production Co-ordinating Committee/J. Howard Miller, artist employed by Westinghouse, US Army/ Lt. Gaetano Faillace; p5 USDOE/National Nuclear Security Administration; p6 Library of Congress/USZ62-49045; p7 US Army; p8 The US National Archives and Records Administration/College Park/Donald R. Ornitz-USHMM, www.auschwitz.org; p10 wikipedia; p11 National Archives of the Netherlands; p12 Everett Collection/Shutterstock; p13 Gary Yim/Shutterstock; p14 The US National Archives and Records Administration/292612; p15 US Army/Lt. Gaetano Faillace; p19 wikispaces/Illingworth, 1946 Daily Mail; p20 US Army/Army Signal Corps/US National Archives; p24 The Hindustan Times, dated 15, 1947; p25t Irisphoto1/Shutterstock, Lefteris Papaulakis/Shutterstock; p26 Galerie Bilderwelt/Bridgeman Images, 26-27 IWM/Royal Air Force/Dowd J (Flying Officer); p28 Harry S. Truman Presidential Library and Museum/Greta Kempton; p29 US Army Air Forces/Margaret Bourke-White; p30 Galerie Bilderwelt/Bridgeman Images; p31t University of Washington/US National Archive, US Navy National Museum of Naval Aviation; p33t Japanese National Railways Foreign Dept., Ocean Yamaha/CCA 2.0 Generic; p34 United Nations Photo; p35 National Archives UK/INF14-447C-543; p37 Seattle Municipal Archives/Engineering Dept. Photographic Negatives Record Series 2613-07/CC 2.0; p38t US Gov, PD/Screenshot from 1952 movie "Duck and Cover"; p39t Neil Armstrong/NASA AS11-40-5948, Cpl. P. McDonald, USMC US Defense Imagery photo VIRIN: 127-GK-234F-A54388; p40 Wikimedia; p41 New York World Telegram and the Sun Newspaper Photograph Collection/Library of Congress/USZ62-128465; p42 US Gov/War Production Co-ordinating Committee/J. Howard Miller, artist employed by Westinghouse; p43 US News and World Report Magazine Photograph Collection/Library of Congress/DIG-ppmsca-03425; p44 US Air Force/SSGT F. Lee Corkran.

t=Top, bl=Bottom Left, br=Bottom Right

Library and Archives Canada Cataloguing in Publication

Seidlitz, Lauri, 1966-, author
    The legacy of World War II / Lauri Seidlitz.

(World War II : history's deadliest conflict)
Includes index.
Issued in print and electronic formats.
ISBN 978-0-7787-2117-8 (bound).--ISBN 978-0-7787-2194-9 (paperback).--
ISBN 978-1-4271-1699-4 (pdf).--ISBN 978-1-4271-1695-6 (html)

    1. Reconstruction (1939-1951)--Juvenile literature. 2. Europe--History--1945- --Juvenile literature. 3. World War, 1939-1945--Peace--Juvenile literature. 4. War crime trials--History--20th century--Juvenile literature. I. Title.

D825.S45 2015   j940.53'14   C2015-904384-0
                                           C2015-904385-9

Library of Congress Cataloging-in-Publication Data

Seidlitz, Lauri.
  The legacy of World War II / Lauri Seidlitz.
      pages cm. -- (World War II: history's deadliest conflict)
  Includes index.
   ISBN 978-0-7787-2117-8 (reinforced library binding) --
  ISBN 978-0-7787-2194-9 (pbk.) --
  ISBN 978-1-4271-1699-4 (electronic pdf) --
  ISBN 978-1-4271-1695-6 (electronic html)
  1. World War, 1939-1945--Influence--Juvenile literature. I. Title.

D743.7.S345 2015
940.53'14--dc23

                                           2015023296

Crabtree Publishing Company

www.crabtreebooks.com   1-800-387-7650

Printed in Canada/112015/EF20150911

Published in Canada
Crabtree Publishing
616 Welland Ave.
St. Catharines, Ontario
L2M 5V6

Published in the United States
Crabtree Publishing
PMB 59051
350 Fifth Avenue, 59th Floor
New York, New York 10118

Published in the United Kingdom
Crabtree Publishing
Maritime House
Basin Road North, Hove
BN41 1WR

Published in Australia
Crabtree Publishing
3 Charles Street
Coburg North
VIC, 3058

CONTENTS

THE GLOBAL WAR DRAWS TO A CLOSE

Timeline

1943

September 8
Italy surrenders to Allied forces

1945

May 8
Germany surrenders
to Allied forces

August 15
Japan surrenders
to Allied forces

World War II (1939–1945) was a true global war that involved almost every country in the world. At the end of the war, only nine countries were **neutral**. The rest had joined with either the **Allied** or **Axis powers**. Allied countries were led by Great Britain, the United States, and the Soviet Union (U.S.S.R. or the United Soviet Socialist Republic). France, Canada, and China were also Allied countries. Axis countries included Germany, Italy, and Japan. Many countries around the world were involved in the war because they were **colonies** of the major powers.

Allied, Axis, and Neutral Countries at the End of World War II

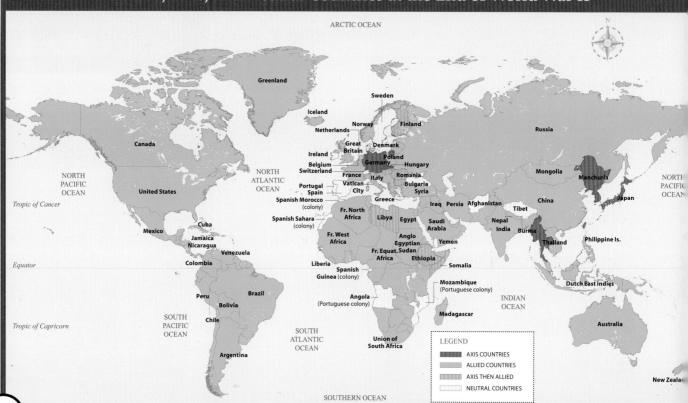

ARCTIC OCEAN

Greenland

Sweden

Iceland

Norway   Finland

Netherlands

Canada   Great   Denmark   Russia
          Britain Poland
Ireland   Belgium Germany Hungary
          Switzerland   Romania   Mongolia
NORTH   France   Italy   Bulgaria
NORTH   ATLANTIC Vatican   Syria   Manchuria
PACIFIC   OCEAN   Portugal City   NORTH
OCEAN   Spain   Greece Iraq Persia Afghanistan China   PACIFIC
Tropic of Cancer Spanish Morocco   Libya Egypt Nepal Tibet Japan OCEAN
United States   (colony) Fr. North   Saudi India Burma
          Spanish Sahara   Africa   Arabia
          (colony)   Yemen   Thailand
Mexico Cuba   Fr. West Anglo   Philippine Is.
        Jamaica   Africa   Egyptian
        Nicaragua   Fr. Equat. Sudan
          Venezuela   Africa Ethiopia
                  Liberia   Somalia
Equator   Colombia Spanish
                   Guinea (colony)   Dutch East Indies
        Peru   Mozambique
             Brazil   Angola (Portuguese colony) INDIAN
        Bolivia   (Portuguese colony)   OCEAN
SOUTH   Chile   Madagascar
PACIFIC
OCEAN   Australia
Tropic of Capricorn
          SOUTH   SOUTH
          Argentina   ATLANTIC Union of
                       OCEAN   South Africa   LEGEND
                                                 ▨ AXIS COUNTRIES
                                                 ▨ ALLIED COUNTRIES
                                                 ▨ AXIS THEN ALLIED
                                                 ▨ NEUTRAL COUNTRIES New Zealand

SOUTHERN OCEAN

END OF THE WAR

In September 1943, Italy surrendered to the Allies. The country had been led by a **dictator** named Benito Mussolini. After years of terrible losses in the war, Mussolini was fired in July 1943. In October, Italy joined the Allies for the rest of the war.

By the spring of 1945, an Allied victory in Europe seemed certain. The leader of **Nazi** Germany was a dictator named Adolf Hitler. Rather than be caught by the Allies, Hitler committed suicide in his underground hiding place on April 30. Two days earlier, Benito Mussolini was shot dead then hung by his feet in Milan, Italy.

On May 8, Germany surrendered to Allied forces. This ended the war in Europe, but the fight in the Pacific between the Allies and Japan continued. In early August 1945, the United States dropped two **nuclear bombs** on the Japanese cities of Hiroshima and Nagasaki. The two bombs killed thousands of people instantly. Others became sick and died in the weeks that followed. Emperor Hirohito of Japan surrendered on August 15. World War II was officially over.

BELOW: *A mushroom cloud erupts from the explosion after the United States dropped a nuclear bomb on Hiroshima.*

> " The war situation has developed not necessarily to Japan's advantage. "
>
> —FROM EMPEROR HIROHITO'S RADIO ADDRESS ANNOUNCING THE SURRENDER OF JAPAN, 1945.

ABOVE: *Austria, May 1945, Hungarian Jews after being removed from Nazi concentration camps to facilities provided by the U.S. Army. Twenty-one million people were homeless or displaced after the war.*

DEVASTATION IN EUROPE

There had never been a war as costly as World War II. For the first time in war history, more **civilians** than soldiers died. Historians estimate that between 35 and 60 million people died in the war. By the end of the war, hundreds of farms, cities, factories, and other facilities were destroyed. European economies were near collapse.

More than 21 million people were homeless. Some had lost their homes in battles. Others had been taken far from their home countries during the war to be used as forced labor. At the end of the war, these **displaced persons** had to find a new place to live or return home. During the summer of 1945, millions of soldiers and civilians tried to make their way home across Europe.

DEVASTATION IN ASIA

Large areas of China were occupied by Japan during the war. The people in these areas suffered greatly under Japanese control. Millions of Chinese people died. More than 60 million were homeless. Many were starving.

Post-war Japan was also in turmoil. About five million Japanese people were wounded, sick, or starving. Nine million people were homeless. Much of the country's wealth was gone.

RIGHT: *Destruction of the Japanese cities Nagasaki (top) and Hiroshima (right) after the United States dropped nuclear bombs.*

CHAPTER 1

WAR CRIMES TRIALS

Timeline

1945

August 8
London Charter of 1945 signed

October 18
Nuremberg Trials begin

1946

April 29
Tokyo War Crimes Trials begin

October 1
Nuremberg Trials end

November 12
Tokyo War Crimes Trials end

On August 8, 1945, the main Allied powers signed the Charter of the International Military Tribunal. This agreement is sometimes known as the London Charter of 1945. The agreement set out how members of the European Axis countries would be tried as criminals for actions during the war.

CONCENTRATION CAMPS

As Allied forces moved into Axis territory at the end of the war, they found thousands of Nazi **concentration camps**. Prisoners at the camps provided slave labor and were executed in large numbers. Conditions in the camps shocked Allied soldiers. They found piles of bodies and mass graves. The prisoners who were still alive were near starvation. Many were so sick that they died soon after they were freed.

BELOW and RIGHT:

Prisoners were liberated from Nazi concentration camps. More than 17 million people were sent to concentration camps during the war.

THE HOLOCAUST

Jewish people were a particular target of the Nazis, who wanted to completely eliminate European Jews. The deliberate Nazi program to wipe out Jewish people and their culture is a **genocide** known as the **Holocaust**.

- At the start of the war, there were nine million Jewish people in Europe.
- By the end of the war, the Nazis had killed more than six million Jews, including 1.5 million Jewish children.
- The Soviet Union lost one million of its Jewish population.
- Almost the entire population of three million Polish Jews were dead.

DISPLACED PERSONS CAMPS

After the war, there were 250,000 Jewish displaced persons. Many did not want to return to their pre-war homes. Many of them lived in camps for displaced persons that were run by the Allied powers. **Zionism** took hold among many Jewish people around the world. Zionism was the desire to form a Jewish homeland in what was then British-controlled Palestine. Jewish people asked Britain to provide territory as a home country.

What do you think?
Why might Jewish displaced persons not want to return home?

> " Each of these pitiful, happy, starved, hysterical men wanted to tell us his home country, his home city, and ask us news and beg for cigarets. [sic] The eyes of these men defy my powers of description. They are the eyes of men who have lived in...horrors for many years, and are now driven half-crazy by the liberation they have prayed so hopelessly for. "

— SIDNEY OLSON, *TIME* MAGAZINE REPORTER FROM DACHAU IN 1945

Nazi Concentration Camp Victims

Jews	6,000,000+
Soviet POWs	3,300,000
Poles	3,000,000
Ukrainians	3,000,000
Belarusians	1,400,000+
Serbs	1,000,000
Romani	232,000
German Mentally or Physically Disabled Patients	232,000
German Political Prisoners	32,000
German Homosexual Men	10,000
Spaniards	9,500
German Blacks	2,000
Jehovah's Witnesses	1,650+

ABOVE: *Jewish people were not the only victims of Nazi programs. Any people the Nazis considered undesirable were sent to concentration camps.*

LEFT: *Defendants sitting in the dock during the Nuremberg Trials. The trials were held in 1945 and tried 22 important Nazi leaders.*

NUREMBERG TRIALS

The desire to try Axis leaders for **war crimes** began during the war. Allied leaders first met to discuss it in 1942. Once the war ended, they discovered the scale of Nazi crimes against Jewish people and other populations. The trials became a certainty. People wanted some form of justice. They needed a way to move on and heal from the horrors of the war.

The International Military Tribunal was held in Nuremberg, Germany, and is known as the Nuremberg Trials. Each of the major Allies—Britain, France, the Soviet Union, and the United States—provided one judge and a **prosecution team**. To convict someone, three of the four judges had to agree.

What do you think?
Do you think it was fair to have judges from only the Allied side? Why or why not?

Beginning on October 18, 1945, the judges heard cases against 22 major Nazi leaders. Some **defendants** argued that they had only been following orders, but this was not accepted as a defense. On October 1, 1946, the judges issued their decisions:

- Twelve defendants were sentenced to death.
- Three defendants received life in prison.
- Four defendants received lesser prison terms.
- Seven defendants were set free.

OTHER WAR CRIMES TRIALS

The court at Nuremberg heard cases against Nazi leaders, who had given the orders and planned to commit mass murder.

Hundreds of other trials were also held in Allied-occupied zones against less important Nazis, including guards, police, army leaders, and doctors who had performed experiments on prisoners.

OUTCOME OF THE TRIALS

Much of what we know today about Nazi war crimes is through evidence given at Nuremburg. The trials raised global awareness about war crimes. They established a **precedent** for holding an international court for crimes of war.

However, not all war criminals were prosecuted. Many resumed their lives in Germany after the war. Some moved to other countries. In some cases, these former Nazis have been found and brought to trial decades after the war.

SIMON WIESENTHAL
(1908–2005)

Simon Wiesenthal was born in what is now Ukraine. He became an architectural engineer. He married his wife, Cyla, in 1936. They lived happily in Poland until the start of the war.

In 1941, Simon and Cyla were sent to a forced labor camp. By August 1942, eighty-nine members of their family had been killed by the Germans. Knowing their lives were in danger, Simon helped Cyla escape.

Simon escaped later in 1943, but was recaptured in 1944. He and many other prisoners were forced on a long march to Austria. By the time he was freed in 1945, he weighed less than 100 pounds (45 kg) and was barely alive.

After the war, he devoted his life to pursuing Nazi war criminals who had escaped prosecution. He and a few others researched the location of Nazis around the globe. Because of their work, 1,100 Nazi criminals were found and put on trial. One of the most famous was Adolf Eichmann, who had organized the Nazi genocide program. Eichmann was arrested in Argentina in 1959. He was found guilty of mass murder and executed in 1961.

About his work, Simon said, "When history looks back, I want people to know the Nazis weren't able to kill millions of people and get away with it."

JAPANESE WAR CRIMES

During the war, Japanese soldiers became known for incredible cruelty toward civilians and prisoners of war (**POWs**). Some people estimate Japanese soldiers killed 10 million Chinese civilians during the war. After the war, some Japanese political and military leaders were charged for war crimes such as the Massacre at Nanking, the Bataan Death March, and the actions of Unit 731.

BELOW: *Japanese soldiers celebrate the capture of Nanking China*

Massacre at Nanking

On December 13, 1937, Japanese soldiers invaded Nanking (now called Nanjing), the capital of China. For six weeks, the soldiers terrorized the city. Thousands of Chinese civilians were robbed and murdered. Girls and women were raped by the soldiers. Homes and businesses were destroyed. Japanese leaders did little or nothing to stop the violence.

Bataan Death March

POWs who survived Japanese captivity told of beatings and random violence. No one had enough food or water. The Bataan Death March is one of the most well-known examples of the mistreatment of POWs. On April 9, 1942, Japanese troops decided to move 70,000 to 80,000 American and Filipino POWs from the Bataan peninsula to a prison about 60 miles (96.5 km) away. On the walk, POWs died from disease, exhaustion, and lack of food and water. Anyone who couldn't keep moving was beaten or killed. About 20,000 people died on the march. Others died after reaching the camp. Approximately 193,000 POWs were held in Japanese camps during World War II. About 27 percent of them died.

Unit 731

Unit 731 was a Japanese army department focused on chemical warfare. The unit was located just outside Harbin, Manchuria, in China. One of its main jobs was to breed germs as weapons. It also experimented with ways of spreading the germs, such as through fleas, rats, gas, and water. The unit tested its weapons on people in nearby Chinese towns and villages. Around 748,000 people died through the unit's experiments. Unit 731 also carried out horrible medical experiments such as cutting people's arms or legs off to see if doctors could reattach them.

LEFT: *Hideki Tojo, former Prime Minister of Japan, shown here sitting between the guards, was sentenced to death during the war trials.*

TOKYO WAR CRIMES TRIALS

At the end of the war, American forces set up a Japanese version of the Nuremberg Trials in Tokyo, Japan. The International Military Tribunal for the Far East had judges from eleven countries. An American judge oversaw the trials. Beginning April 29, 1946, 25 Japanese military and political leaders were put on trial. All were convicted in November of that year.

- Seven defendants were hanged.
- Sixteen defendants were sentenced to life in prison.
- Two defendants received lighter prison sentences.

Ten other countries had their own war crimes trials. Approximately 5,700 Japanese were tried. Of these, 3,000 people were convicted, with 900 of them put to death.

Controversy

Some people thought Emperor Hirohito should have been tried because he had been the ultimate authority in Japan during the war. He had approved the use of chemical weapons. He did nothing to stop the massacre at Nanking. Other members of the royal family were also not tried. General Douglas MacArthur, head of the U.S. forces in Japan, refused to put the emperor on trial. He thought the post-war occupation of Japan would be easier with the emperor's support.

Hirohito insisted he had little power during the war. Others believe he had played an active role in his country's actions. As part of the peace agreement, however, the emperor's role changed. He became a **figurehead** with little political power.

One of the judges at the trial objected to the Tokyo trials. He argued that acts of aggression during the war were not crimes according to international law, so the court had no basis to find people guilty. Some believed the process was biased since the Americans paid for the trials. Still, others argued that the Allies had also committed war crimes, such as dropping nuclear weapons in Japan and destroying the German city Dresden with firebombs. They believed it was unfair to punish only Axis officials.

RIGHT: *Emperor Hirohito and U.S. General Douglas MacArthur met in September 1945.*

What do you think?
Should the Allies also have been punished for war crimes?

CHAPTER 2

POLITICAL AND TERRITORIAL CHANGES POST-WWII

Timeline

1945

July 26
Potsdam Declaration demanding Japanese surrender

Paris Peace Conference begins

October 15
Paris Peace Conference ends

1948

May 14
Israel declares independence

1949

May - October
Germany splits into West Germany and East Germany

1951

September 8
War with Japan officially ended

1955

April 28
American occupation of Japan ends

Changed European Boundaries after World War II

LEGEND

- Germany, pre WWII
- Germany, post WWII
- Alsace-Lorraine - to France post WWII
- Sudetenland - to Czechoslovakia post WWII
- Land to Poland, post WWII

What do you think?

If the Axis powers had won the war, what do you think the map of Europe would look like today?

ABOVE: *After the war, the Allies took control of many German territories. This included Alsace-Lorraine, which went to France, and Sudetenland, which went to Czechoslovakia (now the Czech Republic and Slovakia). Poland received land in eastern Germany, but was forced to give up other land to the Soviets.*

PARIS PEACE TREATIES OF 1947

The Paris Peace Conference was held from July 29, 1946, to October 15, 1946. There, the Allied powers signed peace treaties with Bulgaria, Finland, Hungary, Italy, and Romania. The treaties changed several borders. For example, Italy lost its colonies. Ethiopia and Albania gained independence. Italy also had to give up territory to France, Greece, and Yugoslavia. Hungary lost territory to Bulgaria and Czechoslovakia. Romania lost land to Bulgaria, but gained Transylvania.

FORMATION OF ISRAEL

The Zionist cause, to establish a Jewish homeland, had existed long before World War II. After the war, Zionism gained more support from Western countries. Britain tried to create a Jewish state in Palestine. The Palestinians did not agree. Finally Britain asked the United Nations to settle the matter.

On November 29, 1947, the United Nations voted to divide Palestine into separate Jewish and Arab states. Arab countries, including the majority of the people living in Palestine, objected. On May 14, 1948, the new Jewish state, Israel, declared its independence. The next day, Israel was invaded by Syria, Transjordan (now Jordan), and Egypt. After seven months of fighting, a ceasefire was declared.

RIGHT: *Israel declared its independence in 1948 and gained more land afterward.*

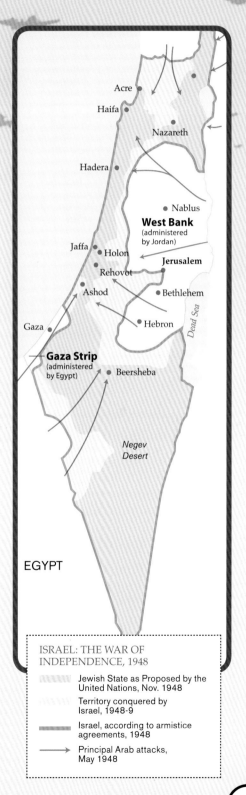

ISRAEL: THE WAR OF
INDEPENDENCE, 1948

Jewish State as Proposed by the United Nations, Nov. 1948

Territory conquered by Israel, 1948-9

Israel, according to armistice agreements, 1948

Principal Arab attacks, May 1948

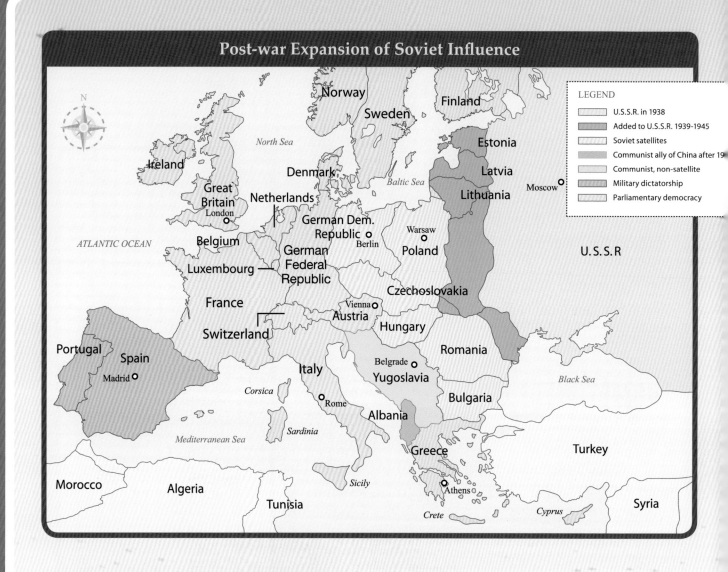

LEGEND

U.S.S.R. in 1938
Added to U.S.S.R. 1939-1945
Soviet satellites
Communist ally of China after 19
Communist, non-satellite
Military dictatorship
Parliamentary democracy

THE IRON CURTAIN DROPS

There were many differences between the Soviet Union and the other Allied countries. The Soviet Union had a communist government. Soviet **communism** supported strong government control of the economy and many other aspects of life. It also supported common ownership of resources and businesses by the whole population. The Soviet Union was ruled by a dictator, Joseph Stalin.

He wouldn't accept any criticism in Soviet society or government.

On the other hand, the United States supported **democracy**, in which a country's citizens have a voice in the government. It also supported **capitalism**, in which private companies operate with as little government involvement as possible.

At the end of the war, relations turned hostile between the Soviet Union and other Allied countries. Europe was soon divided into East and West. The East allied with the Soviet Union. The West allied with the United States. In March 1946, British leader Winston Churchill said an "iron curtain" divided eastern and western Europe.

SOVIET UNION EXTENDS ITS INFLUENCE

In the early years of World War II, the Soviet Union **annexed** three countries along the Baltic Sea: Estonia, Latvia, and Lithuania. After the war, it kept the countries as **Soviet republics**.

In September 1944, Finland signed the Moscow Armistice, which gave a port and a **province** to the Soviets. The Soviets also claimed part of Poland and Czechoslovakia. By 1948, many eastern European countries had become satellites of the Soviet Union. This meant that the countries appeared independent, but the Soviet Union actually controlled their governments.

LEFT: *This 1947 cartoon shows the "curtain" descending across Europe.*

POTSDAM CONFERENCE

The Potsdam Conference was held from July 17 to August 2, 1945, in Potsdam, Germany. It involved the "Big Three" Allied powers: Britain, the United States, and the Soviet Union. The topics were post-war borders, reparations, and goals for the post-war occupation of Axis countries. One goal was to reduce the influence the Nazis had in Germany. The second goal was to remove Germany's military strength. This included taking apart industries that could be used to fight a war. The third goal was to promote democracy.

BELOW: *British Prime Minister Clement Attlee, U.S. President Harry Truman, and Soviet leader Josef Stalin seen at the Potsdam Conference.*

Among the Allies, the Soviet Union had been damaged the most during the war, with 26 million lives lost. It therefore wanted high reparation payments from Germany. A **war reparation** is a payment from the loser of a war to the victor to compensate for damages. However, American and British leaders believed one cause of the war had been high reparation payments imposed on Germany after World War I. They did not want to impose heavy reparations on Germany again. The Soviet Union agreed to smaller reparations than it wanted from Germany. In return, the other Allies agreed to Soviet demands for expanded Polish borders. They also agreed to accept the Soviet-supported Polish government.

Occupation Zones of Post-war Germany, Including Berlin

Denmark

North Sea

Baltic Sea

Former East Prussia

• Hamburg

Danzig

17M

Berlin

Netherlands

22M

German Democratic Republic

Poland

Cologne

Federal Republic of Germany

Bonn

Coblenz

5M

Dresden

• Prague

France

17M

• Nuremburg

Czechoslovakia

• Freiburg

• Munich

Vienna

Switzerland

Austria

Hungary

Italy

LEGEND

American zone
British zone
French zone
Soviet zone
German borders, 1937
Division between East and West Germany
17M Population of occupied zones of Germany (excluding refugees)

ALLIED OCCUPATION

Austria and its capital city, Vienna, were divided into Allied occupation zones. The Allies left in 1955, after signing the Austrian State Treaty. This treaty made Austria independent again. The Allies also divided Germany into zones that were occupied by Britain, France, the Soviet Union, and the United States. Berlin, the capital city, was also divided.

What do you think?
What problems might arise from the way Germany and Berlin were divided?

DIVISION OF EAST AND WEST

In May 1949, the British, French, and American zones in Germany merged. This became the Federal Republic of Germany (West Germany). In October that year, the Soviets formed the German Democratic Republic (East Germany) in its zone. East Germany was communist and dominated by the Soviets. West Germany was democratic and capitalist. Berlin also remained divided into West Berlin (the British, French, and American zones) and East Berlin (the Soviet zone).

POTSDAM DECLARATION

Another outcome of the Potsdam Conference was the Potsdam Declaration, which focused on ending the war with Japan. On July 26, 1945, Great Britain, China, and the United States threatened Japan with "prompt and utter destruction" if it did not surrender. The declaration demanded Japan's unconditional surrender—to disarm, give up all the territories it had gained, and allow the United States to occupy it.

Japan ignored the demands. On August 6, 1945, U.S. President Harry Truman gave the order to drop nuclear bombs on Hiroshima and Nagasaki. The bombs forced Japan's surrender.

DIVISION OF KOREA

The Soviets, looking to expand territory, invaded Korea on August 9, 1945—the same day the United States dropped a nuclear bomb on Nagasaki. In an agreement with the United States, the Soviet Union occupied Korean territory north of the 38th parallel. The Americans occupied the south. The Soviets established a communist government in the north. The Americans set up a democratic, pro-capitalist government in the south.

Both Soviets and Americans wanted to influence events in Korea.

OCCUPATION OF JAPAN

After the war, American troops controlled Japan. General Douglas MacArthur was in charge. The Americans helped write a new **constitution** for Japan, which took effect in May 1947. In the new constitution, the role of the emperor was stripped of political power. Emperor Hirohito stayed emperor, but he became a figurehead with no real power. Japanese women gained the right to vote. Japan gave up the right to declare war, and was allowed only a small military.

The terms of peace were officially set in the Treaty of San Francisco, also known as the Treaty of Peace with Japan, signed on September 8, 1951.

OPPOSITE PAGE: *Japan's territory, at the height of the war, had expanded throughout southeast Asia.*

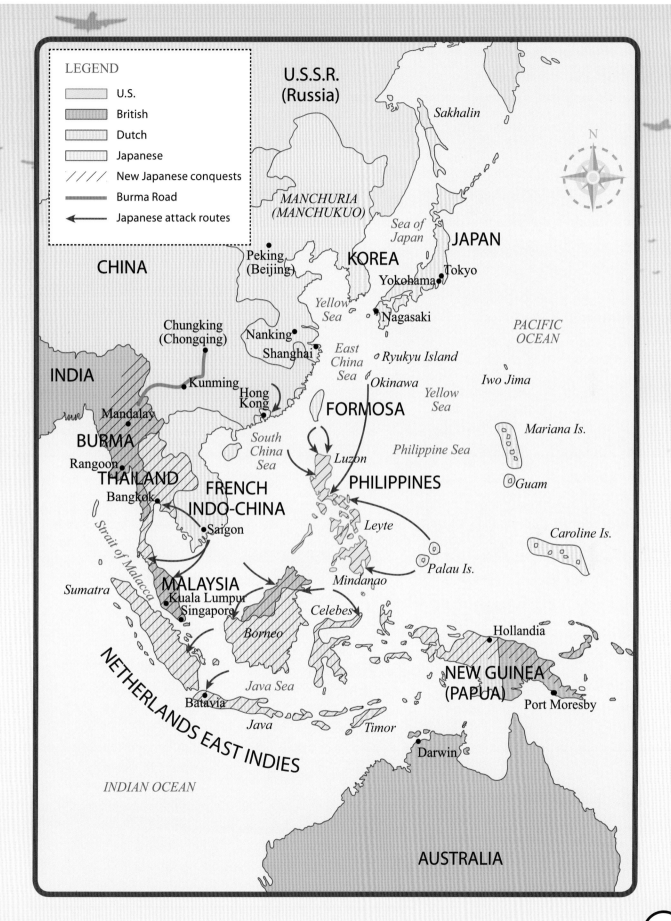

LEGEND
- U.S.
- British
- Dutch
- Japanese
- //// New Japanese conquests
- —— Burma Road
- ← Japanese attack routes

U.S.S.R.
(Russia)

Sakhalin

MANCHURIA
(MANCHUKUO)

CHINA

Peking
(Beijing)

Chungking
(Chongqing)

Nanking

Shanghai

KOREA

Sea of
Japan

JAPAN

Yokohama

Tokyo

Nagasaki

Yellow
Sea

East
China
Sea

PACIFIC
OCEAN

INDIA

Kunming

Mandalay

BURMA

Rangoon

THAILAND

Bangkok

FRENCH
INDO-CHINA

Saigon

Hong
Kong

FORMOSA

Okinawa

Ryukyu Island

Yellow
Sea

Iwo Jima

South
China
Sea

Luzon

PHILIPPINES

Philippine Sea

Mariana Is.

Guam

MALAYSIA

Kuala Lumpur
Singapore

Strait of Malacca

Sumatra

Celebes

Borneo

Leyte

Mindanao

Palau Is.

Caroline Is.

NETHERLANDS EAST INDIES

Java Sea

Batavia

Java

Timor

Hollandia

NEW GUINEA
(PAPUA)

Port Moresby

INDIAN OCEAN

Darwin

AUSTRALIA

N

DECOLONIZATION AFTER WORLD WAR II

Before World War II, many European countries had colonies around the world. They used the resources of their colonies to grow powerful. However, European countries were weak after the war. This encouraged people in the colonies to push forward with demands for **decolonization**, or independence.

In the 25 years following the end of World War II, more than 50 countries gained independence from colonial powers such as Britain, France, and Portugal. Many of those countries were in Africa and southeast Asia. Sometimes independence happened peacefully because many colonial powers could no longer afford to maintain empires. Other times, independence was the result of civil war or rebellion against the colonial power. Many countries suffered years of armed conflict before, during, or after independence.

ABOVE: *Headline of* The Hindustan Times *front page on August 15, 1947, declaring India's independence.*

ABOVE: *Gold Coast Stamp displays Ghana's date of independence: March 6, 1957.*

ABOVE: *Indonesian stamp representing independence from Holland.*

Dates of Independence for Select British and French Colonies

Year of Independence	Colonies
1946	Syria
1946	Jordan
1947	India
1947	Palestine
1948	Lebanon
1948	Burma
1953	Cambodia
1954	Laos
1954	South Vietnam
1956	Tunisia
1956	Sudan
1957	Ghana
1958	Guinea
1960	Central African Republic
1960	Chad
1960	Mali
1960	Niger
1960	Senegal
1960	Nigeria
1960	Somalia
1961	Kuwait
1961	Sierra Leone
1962	Algeria
1962	Uganda
1963	Kenya
1963	Malaysia
1964	Malawi
1964	Tanzania
1964	Zambia
1965	The Gambia
1965	Rhodesia (now Zimbabwe)
1966	Botswana
1966	Lesotho
1967	People's Republic of Yemen
1968	Swaziland

CHAPTER 3

RECONSTRUCTION: EUROPE AND ASIA

Timeline

1941
March 11
Lend-Lease Program approved

December 8
United States enters World War II

1947
Truman Doctrine

Marshall Plan

1948
Deutsche mark becomes new currency in western- occupied Germany

June
Soviets blockade West Berlin

1949
May
Soviets end blockade of West Berlin

October 10
Communist Party declares founding of People's Republic of China

1961
Soviets begin building wall around West Berlin

World War II had been costly on many levels. Millions of people died. In the Soviet Union, 87,000 cities and villages became piles of rubble. Half of the housing was destroyed in many German cities. Italy and France lost about one third of their national wealth. Britain was almost bankrupt. Millions of Europeans struggled to find food, shelter, friends, and family.

BELOW: *Large areas of many European cities were reduced to rubble during the war.*

RIGHT: *The German city of Hamburg was bombed heavily during the war.*

FEAR OF COMMUNISM

After the war, the United States believed it could not ignore Europe. If it did, the economic devastation from the war might lead to the spread of communism. This would allow the Soviet Union to gain more power and influence. Communism promised a strong government and a basic standard of living, and often appealed to people living in extreme poverty.

The United States wanted to expand its own influence and power. During the war, the United States had supported the other Allies with supplies of food and resources, under a program called the Lend-Lease Program. The program ensured countries were friendly to American interests. However, this program ended when the war was over. A new plan was required to ensure that the United States would not lose influence in Europe.

MARSHALL PLAN

In 1947, U.S. Secretary of State George Marshall proposed a plan to help rebuild Europe and spread American influence. The European Recovery Plan (known as the Marshall Plan) was in place from 1948 to 1952. Through it, the United States provided $13 billion and machinery and supplies to the war-ravaged European countries. The aid was very successful. By 1950, Western Europe had returned its industrial strength almost to pre-war levels. Germany, Italy, and other western European countries had become firm allies of the United States.

HARRY TRUMAN
(1884–1972)

Harry Truman grew up on a farm in Independence, Missouri. His family couldn't afford to send him to college, so he worked a variety of jobs after high school.

Harry served as a captain in France during World War I. After the war, he started a hat shop. However, when the business failed in 1922, Harry vowed to repay all the money he owed. It took him 15 years to clear his debts.

He was elected U.S. Senator in 1934. He became known as an **ethical** man. In 1945, he was elected as President Franklin Roosevelt's vice president. Then, just 82 days after taking office again, Roosevelt died of a stroke. Suddenly Harry Truman was sworn in as president at a turning point in history.

He soon announced the German surrender in World War II, and made the decision to sign the United Nations Charter. He also made the decision to drop atomic bombs on Japan to force its surrender. Harry had a sterner view of communism than Roosevelt had. His firm line against communist expansion helped start the **Cold War**.

TRUMAN DOCTRINE

In 1947, U.S. President Harry Truman changed American **foreign policy** to respond to the growing Soviet influence. The Truman Doctrine was a policy in which the United States took an active role in preventing the spread of communism. The doctrine was a huge change from the pre-war isolation of the United States.

> " In this period of transition we must make sure that the victory that has been won—won by the effort of all the people and at a cost of a million casualties—does not slip from our grasp... We must not shirk the task of enforcing the surrender of Germany and Japan, including the occupation of the hostile areas allotted to us as our share of the responsibility, for as long a time as may prove to be necessary. "
>
> —U.S. SECRETARY OF WAR,
> ROBERT P. PATTERSON, SEPTEMBER 27, 1945

What do you think?
How does the quotation from Robert P. Patterson foreshadow the Marshall Plan?

The Truman Doctrine was first used in 1947 in Greece and Turkey. Truman believed that allowing Greece and Turkey to become communist would lead to war in the whole region. The United States agreed to send $400 million to help Greece and Turkey recover and to stop the communists.

REBUILDING GERMANY

Shift in Policy

The Allies' initial plan after the war was to tear apart Germany's industries. They wanted to stop Germany from going to war again. However, fear of Soviet expansion in Europe forced the western Allies to change their minds. The Germans in the occupied zones were eager for changes. Day-to-day survival was hard enough. The Germans submitted to Allied occupation without protest. The western Allies began to see Germany as a possible ally against the Soviets.

German Economic Miracle

The western Allies realized that the recovery of the German economy was critical to recovery throughout the rest of Europe. They began to help Germany rebuild. In 1948, the Deutsche mark became the new currency in West Germany. This currency helped the economy. In 1949, the Marshall Plan was extended to West Germany. West Germany received about $1.45 billion in loans from the United States from 1949 to 1952.

West Germany rebuilt its factories. By the late 1950s, West Germany again had one of the world's strongest economies. People called this the "German Economic Miracle" because it had happened so quickly.

RIGHT: *Destroyed German factories shown in 1945. Many factories were rebuilt and running again by the late 1950s.*

ABOVE: *Citizens watching a plane land in Berlin during 1948 airlift. The Berlin Airlift provided 2.3 million tons of supplies to West Berlin.*

Berlin Blockade

The Soviets were angered by the Marshall Plan and efforts to rebuild Germany. After all, they had been invaded by Germany in two recent world wars. They did not want to see Germany united and strong. In addition, the Soviets feared the growth of American influence. On June 23, 1948, the Soviets blockaded West Berlin, preventing people and goods from moving in or out. They hoped they could force West Berlin to surrender to Soviet control.

The western Allies responded with the Berlin Airlift. Until May 1949, when the blockade was lifted, Allied planes dropped food and fuel in to help West Berlin.

Berlin Wall

West Berlin was an embarrassment to the Soviets. Thousands of East Germans crossed the border to the West and never returned. In June 1961, the Soviet Union built a wall around West Berlin. The Berlin Wall was 12 feet (3.6 m) tall and 4 feet (1.2 m) wide and watched by heavily armed guards and dogs. More than 171 people died trying to cross the border.

RIGHT: *The Berlin wall was built by the Soviets around West Berlin.*

BELOW: *Planes from the United States unloading supplies in Berlin during the blockade.*

POST-WAR JAPAN

Japan was no better off than Europe after the war. It had lost more than one third of its industries and about 25 percent of its national wealth. Six million Japanese people were displaced from China, Korea, and other countries as Japan gave up its occupied territories. More than 100,000 people died after the American bombing of Hiroshima and Nagasaki, and survivors suffered illness for years.

Rebuilding

At first, the American occupation of Japan focused on punishing the Japanese. The United States wanted Japan to never again attack other countries. The Marshall Plan was not offered to Japan. Economic recovery was left to the Japanese. However, by 1948, the Allies worried that without economic growth, Japan might become a communist country. The United States decided that rebuilding Japan was the best way to spread American influence throughout East Asia.

By 1949, the Americans were focused on rebuilding Japan's economy. They did not ask for war reparations. Japan's economy was helped by tax reforms and stable costs of goods. The biggest problem, however, was finding markets for Japanese goods.

The outbreak of the Korean War soon provided a solution. Japan became the main supplier of goods to the United Nations' forces in Korea. The demand for supplies helped economic growth. By the 1950s, Japan was on the road to economic recovery. Japan was a strong ally of the United States long after Japan regained much of its independence in the 1950s. The United States continued to occupy Iwo Jima until 1968, and Okinawa until 1972. Some American military troops still remain in Japan today at the invitation of the government.

High-tech Economy

Japan was only allowed a small military force after the war. It was forced to depend on the United States for defense. The money Japan saved on defense was put toward its economy. The Japanese built new factories with modern technology. Japan's manufacturing and electronics industries quickly became among the best in the world. In the 1960s and 1970s, Japan's economy grew rapidly. It sold goods such as cars and electronics around the world. By the 1980s, it was one of the richest countries in the world.

Super-speed services on the New Tokaido Line are commenced on October 1st.

OCT 1964						
S	M	T	W	T	F	S
...	...	...	...	1	2	3
4	5	6	7	8	9	10
11	12	13	14	15	16	17
18	19	20	21	22	23	24
25	26	27	28	29	30	31

NOV 1964						
S	M	T	W	T	F	S
1	2	3	4	5	6	7
8	9	10	11	12	13	14
15	16	17	18	19	20	21
22	23	24	25	26	27	28
29	30	...	...	...	...	...

DEC 1964						
S	M	T	W	T	F	S
...	...	1	2	3	4	5
6	7	8	9	10	11	12
13	14	15	16	17	18	19
20	21	22	23	24	25	26
27	28	29	30	31		

RIGHT: *This is a Honda car from the 1960s. Car manufacturing became a large part of the post-war Japanese economy.*

CHAPTER 4

FOUNDING THE UNITED NATIONS

Timeline

1942

January 1
Declaration of the
United Nations

1945

February 4–11
Yalta Conference

June 26
Charter of the
United Nations signed

The first international organization was the League of Nations. It was created after World War I. It was supposed to keep peace and avoid future wars. However, it did not work well, and it did not prevent World War II. After the war, the Allied countries wanted to create a better international organization.

RIGHT: *The UN World Charter was signed by 50 nations on June 26, 1945.*

DECLARATION OF THE UNITED NATIONS

The name "United Nations" was first used at a meeting during the war in 1941. People from 26 Allied countries met in Washington, DC, to discuss the war. On January 1, 1942, they signed the Declaration of the United Nations. In this document, each country promised to continue to work together to fight the Axis powers. Later that year, the United States and Britain planned for "a general international organization based on the principle of sovereign equality of all nations."

CHARTER OF THE UNITED NATIONS

Representatives from 50 nations met in San Francisco from April to June 1945. They signed the Charter of the United Nations there.

The four main goals of the United Nations are:
- to keep peace
- to help nations work together
- to promote human rights
- to plan international activities

The General Assembly includes all member nations. It is the main forum for discussions. The UN also has a Security Council. The Security Council meets whenever peace is in danger. The council has five permanent members: the United States, the United Kingdom (Britain), China, the Russian Federation (formerly the Soviet Union), and France. There are also nine other rotating members.

Excerpt from the Preamble to the Charter of the United Nations:

We the peoples of the United Nations determined
- to save succeeding generations from the scourge of war, which twice in our lifetime has brought untold sorrow to mankind, and
- to reaffirm faith in fundamental human rights, in the dignity and worth of the human person, in the equal rights of men and women and of nations large and small, and
- to promote social progress and better standards of life in larger freedom.

What do you think?

Why do you think the leaders of Britain, the Soviet Union, and the United States believed the permanent members of the Security Council should have a **veto**?

RIGHT: *At the Yalta Conference in February 1945, Churchill, Roosevelt, and Stalin agreed that each of the five permanent members of the Security Council would have a veto.*

CHAPTER 5

THE COLD WAR

Timeline

1957
October
Sputnik launched

1959
January
Castro leads revolution in Cuba

1961
April
Bay of Pigs

1962
October
Cuban Missile Crisis

1969
July
Apollo 11 lands on the moon

1980's
October 1985
Mikhail Gorbachev becomes leader of the Soviet Union

November 1989
Berlin wall was opened

1990
October
East Germany and West Germany reunited

1991
Soviet Union collapses

The relationship between the Soviet Union and the rest of the Allied powers fell apart at the end of World War II. The Soviet Union wanted to spread communism across the world. The United States wanted to spread its own influence, including global capitalism. Countries quickly divided into two camps: East (communist) and West (capitalist).

SUPERPOWERS AND THE COLD WAR

After World War II, a new type of war began: the Cold War. The Cold War was waged between the two **superpowers** that emerged at the end of World War II: the United States and the Soviet Union. Britain, France, and Germany no longer dominated world affairs after the war. They focused on rebuilding their countries.

The United States, however, had taken little damage in the war. Its cities and towns were strong and healthy. In fact, the American economy was booming. Building arms for the war had helped its economy. After the war, the United States entered a period of great prosperity.

OPPOSITE PAGE: *Seattle's Alaska Way viaduct was under construction in 1952. Many American highways and new homes were built when the economy boomed in the post-war years.*

SOVIET EXPANSION

Stalin had supported democracy at meetings with Allied leaders during and after the war. At first, Soviet interference with other Eastern European countries was hard to detect. For example, these countries had elections. However, the Soviets prevented anyone other than communists from winning. Some elections had only one person on the ballot: a communist.

The United States offered the Marshall Plan to all European countries. The Soviets knew the plan would increase American power. So they stopped countries in Eastern Europe from accepting the plan. In 1947 and 1948, many of these countries became communist with Soviet support, including Bulgaria, Czechoslovakia, Hungary, Poland, Romania, and Yugoslavia.

THE CIA AND THE COLD WAR

The Cold War was "cold" because the Soviet Union and United States didn't directly go to battle with each other. The war instead involved **espionage**, political pressure, **propaganda**, and **proxy wars**.

The Central Intelligence Agency (CIA) was formed on September 18, 1947. The CIA's job is to gather information from around the world about threats to the United States. The CIA also interferes in the affairs of other countries to protect American interests. The CIA and the Soviet intelligence agency, the KGB, played key roles in the Cold War.

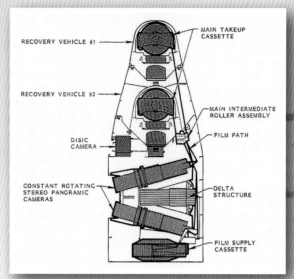

ABOVE: *This corona satellite was used by the CIA for spying on the Soviets.*

ABOVE: *"Duck and Cover" was a 1952 film, teaching children to take cover during a nuclear attack.*

ARMS RACE

One of the biggest threats to world peace during the Cold War was the **arms race**. At first, only the United States had nuclear weapons. After the Soviet Union exploded its first nuclear weapon in 1949, both superpowers raced to build as many weapons as possible, spending billions to prevent an attack from the other side. Since both sides could destroy the other with their weapons, neither side would attack first.

SPACE RACE

On October 4, 1957, the Soviet Union launched Sputnik, the first **satellite** to be sent into space. The United States wasn't happy to see the Soviets get ahead in the **space race**. Each superpower wanted to be better than the other. In 1958, the United States launched its first satellite. It also formed the National Aeronautics and Space Administration (NASA). From then on, the two countries competed for new achievements in space. On July 20, 1969, the United States became the first country to land people on the moon, and a gradual decline began in the space race.

ABOVE: *The United States was the first nation to land people on the moon on July 20, 1969.*

Sputnik is the Russian word for "traveler".

KOREAN WAR

The Korean War was a proxy war, which is a war started by major powers that do not actually enter the war. Powerful countries, such as the United States or Soviet Union, instead support the countries fighting, with advice, weapons, and other supplies.

In June 1950, North Korea invaded South Korea by crossing the divide set up in 1948 by the United States and the Soviet Union. By July, the United Nations (without the Soviet Union) agreed to help South Korea. The United States, Canada, and six other countries all sent troops. Communist China sent troops to help North Korea. By 1953, the war was over. Five million people had died and the country remained split.

ABOVE: *UN forces seen defending South Korea in the Korean War.*

ABOVE: *The 1961 invasion of Cuba at the Bay of Pigs failed.*

COLD WAR HEATS UP IN CUBA

On January 1, 1959, Fidel Castro led a successful movement to overthrow the Cuban government led by General Fulgencio Batista. Batista was a dictator, and he was friendly to the United States. Castro wanted a communist Cuban government instead.

The U.S. government and CIA tried to push Castro from power. By 1960, Castro and the Soviet Union had developed a strong relationship. The United States was worried about having a Soviet ally so close to the country's coast. In April 1961, the CIA secretly launched an invasion of Cuba, using Cuban **exiles** living in Miami. They attacked the Bay of Pigs on Cuba's south shore. It was a complete disaster. In less than 24 hours, the invading force had been defeated.

Cuban Missile Crisis

In July 1962, the United States discovered that nuclear missile sites were being built in Cuba. U.S. President John F. Kennedy ordered the U.S. navy to stop Soviet ships from getting to Cuba. Kennedy threatened Soviet Premier Nikita Khrushchev. Neither leader wanted a war, but neither believed they could back down or show weakness.

By October 26, war seemed impossible to avoid. The crisis ended on October 28 through secret conversations between Kennedy and Khrushchev. The United States promised not to invade Cuba again. In return, the Soviets would not place nuclear missiles on the island.

After the Cuban Missile Crisis, a "hotline" was put in the U.S. president's office and Soviet premier's office. This telephone link meant the two leaders could call each other to solve problems.

THE COLD WAR ENDS

Both superpowers were scared by how close to a nuclear war they had come in 1962. In 1969, they began negotiations to slow down the arms race. In 1972 and 1979, the United States and the Soviet Union signed Strategic Arms Limitation treaties (SALT I and SALT II). The treaties marked the beginning of the end of the Cold War.

ABOVE: *American marchers deliver messages to Kennedy during the Cuban Missile Crisis. The signs are warning Kennedy to be careful and make peace.*

CHAPTER 6

WOMEN'S RIGHTS

Timeline

1946

Japanese women gain the right to vote

1964

Women's rights added to the U.S. Civil Rights Act

1970

Royal Commission on the Status of Women makes recommendations on improving women's equality in Canada

During World War II, men in both Allied and Axis countries were **drafted** into the military. This meant they were forced by law to fight in the war. As more and more men left, employers had trouble filling their jobs. They depended on women to fill the men's positions.

RIGHT: *This poster of "Rosie the Riveter" is one used by the United States government to encourage women to go to work in factories. These factories would build war supplies.*

What do you think?
How is this poster an example of propaganda?

Once the men left for war, women kept family businesses running. Other women took paid jobs in factories. By 1945, approximately three million women in the United States worked outside the home. Many built ships, planes, and weapons. Others worked in the military as nurses or truck drivers. In Canada, more than 50,000 women enlisted in the Canadian army, navy, and air force.

In the Axis countries, fewer women worked outside the home. In Germany, for example, slave labor by prisoners reduced the need for women to take on jobs.

BELOW: *March for women's rights in Washington, DC, in 1970*

RISE OF THE WOMEN'S RIGHTS MOVEMENT

After the war, women's wartime jobs were given to returning soldiers. Some women did not want to give up the independence they had gained during the war. Many women had new ideas about what they were able to do, and they resisted the return to traditional roles.

In the 1960s, this fight became the Women's Rights Movement. Women demanded the right to work in all kinds of jobs. They also wanted to be paid the same as men. In 1964, women's protection from discrimination was included in the Civil Rights Act in the United States. In Canada in 1970, the Royal Commission on the Status of Women made 167 recommendations for ways to improve women's equality in Canada.

CONCLUSION

In March 1985, Mikhail Gorbachev became leader of the Soviet Union. He hoped to reform his country to be more open. His reforms began a dramatic period of change. By 1991, the communist governments of many Eastern European countries were gone. Some of the Soviet republics demanded independence. In December 1991, the Soviet Union was replaced by the Commonwealth of Independent States. The Cold War was over.

RIGHT: *In November 1989, the Berlin Wall was opened and the people began tearing it down. On October 3, 1990, East and West Germany were formally united for the first time since World War II.*

LEGACIES OF WORLD WAR II

World War II caused many changes in the world. The desire to avoid future wars resulted in the creation of the United Nations. Colonies demanded and achieved independence. Europe lost power. The United States and the Soviet Union gained power. Nuclear weapons were stockpiled as East and West competed for global dominance. A new set of conflicts and the Cold War were just two of the many legacies of World War II.

FURTHER READING AND WEBSITES

BOOKS

Grant, Reg. *World War II: the events and their impact on real people*. DK Publishing, 2008.

Jeffrey, Gary. *North Africa and the Mediterranean*. Crabtree Publishing Company, 2012.

Jeffrey, Gary. *The Eastern Front*. Crabtree Publishing Company, 2012.

Jeffrey, Gary. *War in the Pacific*. Crabtree Publishing Company, 2012.

Keegan, John. *Atlas of World War II*. Collins, 2006.

Kennedy, David M., ed. *World War II Companion*. Simon & Schuster, 2007.

Overy, Richard, ed. *The Times Atlas of the 20th Century*. Times Books, 1996.

Story, Ronald. *Concise Historical Atlas of World War Two: The Geography of Conflict*. Oxford University Press, 2005.

WEBSITES

The History Channel, with sections for American and Canadian History
http://www.history.com/topics

Milestones in the History of U.S. Foreign Relations
https://history.state.gov/milestones

World War II
Images, audio and video clips, an interactive map, and quizzes.
http://www.britannica.com/ EBchecked/topic/648813/ World-War-II

AUTHOR BIOGRAPHY

Lauri Seidlitz has been an editor and writer for more than 20 years. She has edited a number of textbooks in science, history, and social studies, including an award-winning series of First Nations studies textbooks. She is the author of several books for students, and currently teaches editing classes at the University of Calgary. She holds a master's degree in English, and undergraduate degrees in English and political science.

GLOSSARY

Allied powers a group of countries that fought together during World War II, led by Britain, France, the Soviet Union, and the United States

annex to forcefully take control of a territory

arms race a competition between countries to have the best and most weapons

Axis powers a group of countries that fought together during World War II, led by Germany, Italy, and Japan

capitalism an economic system in which resources and businesses are all or mostly privately owned; involves competition and profit

civilian person who is not in the armed forces

Cold War a war waged between the Soviet Union and United States after World War II. They didn't directly go to battle with each other. The war instead involved espionage, political pressure, propaganda, and proxy wars.

colony a country controlled by a stronger country that uses the colony's resources for its own benefit

communism a social and economic system founded on the idea that society as a whole, through its government, should own resources and businesses; results in a large, strong government

concentration camp a prison where people were forced to work for the Nazi war effort and/or executed

constitution the document that outlines the system of laws by which a country is governed

decolonization the process of making a colony or a group of colonies independent

defendant a person who is accused of a crime in a court of law

democracy a system of government in which citizens have a voice, either directly or through representatives

dictator a leader who has complete authority over a country

displaced persons people who have been forced away from their homeland

drafted to be forced by law to join a country's armed forces

espionage spying on enemy countries

ethical describing a person who tries to follow good or moral rules of behavior

exiles people who can no longer live in their homeland, usually for political reasons

figurehead a person who is called the head or chief of something but who has no real power

foreign policy a country's goals for its relations with other countries

genocide the deliberate killing of all members of a particular ethnic group

Holocaust the systematic Nazi program to wipe out European Jewish people and their culture

Nazis a political party in Germany that promoted German pride, the belief that Germany had been unfairly treated after World War I, and strong anti-Jewish beliefs

neutral not involved and not supporting one side or the other

nuclear bombs powerful explosive devices first developed and used at the end of World War II

POW stands for prisoner of war; a soldier or civilian captured by the opposing side in a war

precedent something that can be used as an example or rule to be followed in the future

propaganda information designed to influence people's ideas, emotions, and actions in specific ways

prosecution team the legal team that argues that the person accused of the crime is guilty

province areas that some countries are divided into, similar to states

proxy war a war started by major powers that do not actually enter the war. Major powers instead provide advice, weapons, and supplies to the fighting countries.

Romani an ethnic group that traditionally moved from place to place, living on the edges of European and American settlements

satellite a country that is formally independent, but is really under another country's control; also an object that orbits a planet

Soviet republic individual communist states that belonged to the Soviet Union

space race a competition between countries to be first in space exploration

superpower a country that is powerful enough to influence world affairs in its own interests

veto the right to reject a decision by a law-making body

war crime a crime that violates the customs of war, such as murdering civilians, mistreating soldiers, and destroying property not required by military need

war reparation a payment from the loser of a war to the victor to compensate for damages and other costs

Zionism a movement to establish a homeland for Jewish people near Jerusalem. The movement gained worldwide support after the Holocaust.

INDEX